THIS
BOOK
BELONGS
TO:

Made in the USA
Monee, IL
15 March 2023

29962708R00060